THE
Archive Photographs
SERIES

MALDON
AND
HEYBRIDGE

THE
Archive Photographs
SERIES

MALDON
AND
HEYBRIDGE

Compiled by
Patrick Lacey

First published 1996

The Chalford Publishing Company
St Mary's Mill, Chalford,
Stroud, Gloucestershire, GL6 8NX

ISBN 0 7524 0648 5

Typesetting and origination by
The Chalford Publishing Company
Printed in Great Britain by
Redwood Books, Trowbridge

Contents

Acknowledgements

I wish to thank the Trustees of the Maldon District Museum for permission to use their photographic collection and to the Essex Record Office for permission to publish the four photographs marked E.R.O. in the text.

The help of John and June Prime of the Maldon Society Photographic Archive, John Came, Wendy Came, Betty Chittenden, George Ginn, John Osborne, Doreen Penneck and Tony Wright was much appreciated.

Special thanks are due to Joanne Maynard for word-processing and to my wife Pamela for ensuring that everything was kept in order.

The Maldon District Museum will benefit from the proceeds of the sale of this book.

Introduction

Maldon is unusual in being a Saxon hill town situated on the east side of England on a river estuary. Recent excavations have revealed an extensive Romano-British town on low lying ground near Heybridge but this was largely abandoned by the beginning of the fifth century. The Saxons established their village nearby on higher ground which was less liable to flood but retained its maritime connections.

Since the Battle of Maldon in 991 between the Saxons and the Vikings, which was chronicled in a poem in early English, the town has enjoyed a generally peaceful existence. It reached a peak of prosperity in the eighteenth century as fashionable facades were added to older buildings in its principal streets and local merchants prospered from the growing trade in the timber and agricultural products with London and Continental ports. However in 1796 a blow was struck against the port of Maldon by the decision to route the Navigation, formed of canalised rivers, around it to gain entry into the Blackwater estuary at Heybridge Basin. New industries were attracted into Heybridge by the ease of transport this provided causing this small village to expand and flourish.

The arrival of the railway in Maldon in 1848 encouraged further industrial development to an area already occupied by lime kilns, wharf's, timber yards and a tannery. These activities had previously been dependent on water transport, particularly the Thames Sailing Barge. Iron foundries, concentrating on the manufacture of agricultural equipment, were established. By this time the town was lit by gas, supplied from a gas works in the High Street.

In the countryside, steam power, in the form of portable and traction engines, eased work on the farm. Farm implements produced by local firms starting with improved ploughs and cultivators but moving onto turnip cutters, chaff cutters and root pulpers, were adopted by the farming community, reducing the difficulty of various tasks and increasing productivity.

Electricity was provided to customers in the town by John Sadd, timber merchants, in the early years of the twentieth century. The technology of milling advanced and roller mills powered by electricity, generated by steam, superceded the ancient water driven grinding mills. These new mills were still erected at waterside locations for ease of transport. Their owners tended to live close to their sites of work and, as their businesses prospered, they could contribute increasingly to the civic and religious life of Maldon and Heybridge. Less is known of the working people of the area but, because of the expansion of industry, there was less poverty and homelessness than in some other Essex towns.

By the 1890s the population had more opportunity for leisure and mass tourism had begun.

Maldon became a popular day trip destination for many living near London. Soon automobiles were becoming an increasingly common sight with some being built in Heybridge. Apart from in times of war, seasonal visitors have continued to be attracted to the area until the present day.

The Maldon Borough Museum was founded in 1923 by a group of interested councillors and was housed in a room above the fire station in London Road. The station was rebuilt in 1938 and the old building which included the museum room was demolished. The contents of the museum were put into storage, from which they did not emerge for thirty years when Mrs Cath Backus, helped by Mrs Maisie Woodward, ex-mayor of Maldon, rescued them. Cath Backus became the Chairman of the Maldon Museum Association, a post which she was to occupy for twenty-five years and it was through her efforts that the museum exists today. Since re-establishment in 1968, the museum has held its premises on an annual lease, first above Matthew's, corn chandlers shop in the High Street and more recently at 'Spindles', the charming cottage in Church Walk which was the home and business premises of Maisie Woodward for many years.

Two further storage periods have occurred but now, hopefully, a permanent home has been found at the Lodge House on the Promenade. It seemed an appropriate time to produce a record of some of the photographic collection belonging to the museum. The collection consists mostly of local postcards but is supplemented by family photographs, which have been donated to the museum. Whilst Cath Backus was Chairman, the museum followed a gruelling programme of exhibitions of local and general interest, changing every eight to ten weeks. Some of the excellent photographs used in these exhibitions were retained in the collection while other postcards have been loaned by friends of the museum, whose help is acknowledged elsewhere in this book.

The postcards mostly date from between 1900 to 1914, when they were used as the primary means of communication between separated family members. The 2,600 troops who attended an annual camp near Maldon in 1913 sent 14,926 personal letters and postcards through the YMCA in the first week alone, an average of over five communications per person! Many of these were local picture postcards bearing such images as the local police station, workhouse and borough cemetery as well as those of nearby beauty spots.

In looking at the postcards one must beware of deducing too much from the scene depicted. One card suggests that, because of lack of road traffic, boys were allowed to play football in the High Street. However the local newspaper from the time shows that summonses had been issued against five lads for playing football on the highway. On appearing before local magistrates they were each fined one shilling.

The earliest photographs shown date from the 1870s and the most recent from the 1970s, giving an account of life in and around the area for nearly a century. There is much more to be learned about these illustrations of a period of such change and I hope this book will prompt more faces from the past to be recognised and more information to be obtained.

One

From Maldon East to Market Hill

For over one hundred years, until the station's closure in September 1964, the most usual way of arriving in Maldon was by train from Witham. This driver's eye view shows, from left to right, the goods handling shed, the level crossing posts, the engine shed in the distance, the station platforms and quaint crossing keeper's cottage with its decorative chimney. The strangely shaped building on the far right was known as the balloon shed although it never served this purpose at Maldon, being erected on this site after the First World War.

Driver Mitton leans from the cab of one of the diesel units which replaced the steam trains in 1956 and hands the token, which has allowed him to proceed down the single track branch, to the waiting signal man.

Signal man Ernest Bowles operates the signal lever in the large signal box, which controls all movements of trains in the station area and up the branch.

This splendid view by Mr H. Springett shows great activity in the goods yard in the 1950s. Agricultural products and machinery are being loaded whilst coal is placed in sacks to supply the town. The station in Maldon had drawn manufacturing industry to the area since the line opened in 1848. Beyond the goods yard can be seen the piles of timber in Sadd's premises.

The large work force of the station, goods yard and motive power depot at Maldon shown in the early 1950s under the arched porticoes of Maldon East station.

In 1958 the line was worked by diminutive railbuses, the first of which is being admired here on its entry into service.

This remarkable photograph was discovered by Mr Barry Beardall and presented to the Maldon Museum in 1970, but it must have been taken almost a century earlier. The locomotive was built in 1873 but its train of carriages date back to the beginning of services in the 1850s. Shunting wagons by horse was not uncommon and would have been very useful in moving them on to the rails of the nearby quay.

This turn of the century view shows the handsome facade of the station together with some of the staff and the horse bus of the Kings Head, which would convey passengers up the steep Market Hill to their accommodation. This, and a similar vehicle owned by the Blue Boar, would meet every train, but on request would call at any part of the town for a fare of 6d in 1906.

From the station gates can be seen the premises of the Railway Bell selling fine ales brewed by the Chelmsford brewery. Beyond is Barritt's wharf, where hay and straw were loaded into sailing barges to supply the horse population of London. To the right are the Rayleigh Roller mills which were built in 1896 by Samuel Garratt who had previously owned Hoe mills in Woodham Walter.

A postcard dated November 1905 from a gentleman working at Sadd's shows Station Road busy with horse-drawn vehicles. The extension to the station awnings can be seen in contrast to the view on page 13.

The development of steam mills with river frontage, which allowed ready import of foreign wheat for milling in addition to that locally grown, was to spread doom for the many inland water mills. In 1916 Garratt's mill was purchased by William Green whose mill at Raydon had been burnt down - a not uncommon fate at the time. The building shown was lit by electricity from the time of its erection and had the most up-to-date milling equipment installed.

A photograph showing the river frontage before the construction of Rayleigh roller mill in 1896. On the river bank is the lime kiln which together with the adjacent coalyard belonged to Rutt, Gutteridge and Company.

A continuation of the previous view shows the premises of B.F. Joslin, stone mason and opposite is the brick building erected by Messrs Bentall Brothers as a nuts and bolts factory but converted by Oliver Belsham in 1891 to be a roller flour mill. The lime kilns, stonemasons and flour mills were all dependent on the Thames sailing barge for transport. An early example with its Thames lighter stern and tiller steering is seen in the dock.

A sailing barge at Green's mill, c.1900 seen from the Down's footpath. Over two thousand of these useful craft were registered at the time. In Maldon they belonged to the Sadd, Keeble and Strutt families.

A scene showing Maldon iron works, built in 1875 by Joseph Warren and, in the background, signals and signal box on the Great Eastern Railway.

Joseph Warren moved his foundry from Broad Street Green to Maldon in the 1850s, attracted by the possibility of transporting his products easily by rail and water and erected this fine building in 1875. The factory concentrated on the production of agricultural implements but also produced the cast iron direction posts used throughout Essex. Close to the ironworks stood the Foundry House for the owner and the twelve cottages of Foundry Terrace for the employees.

The river, at this point the Chelmer rather than the Blackwater, seen from Fullbridge. The lime kiln is clearly visible on the right with Sadd's timber wharf in the far distance on the left.

Sadd's owned a fleet of spritsail barges and lighters to transfer cargoes of imported timber to the wharf from larger vessels lying off Osea Island. Before 1851 packet boats ran a weekly service to London from this wharf.

Vessels up to 300 tons could lie alongside the wharf. Here a vessel is being unloaded with two tiller steered sailing barges in attendance.

Sadd's were able to burn sawdust and off cuts which produced gas to fuel engines which in turn generated electricity for their own works in 1909 and to supply Maldon and Heybridge with 220VDC from 1912-1931. Generating equipment is shown here.

Rafts of timber lie floating in the River Blackwater. Sadd's stored timber in this way here and in the long pond, a railway dock which was dug alongside Maldon East station in 1848 but was never used.

Maldonians and their dogs exercising on the ice at Fullbridge in January 1892. The winters from 1890 to 1892 were extremely severe with many vessels being trapped in the ice. Skating was possible at Fullbridge and along the thirteen mile stretch of canal to Springfield, near Chelmsford.

A disastrous fire destroyed the steam powered saw mill at Sadd's in 1909. The sawmill was replaced by two buildings: one for logs and the other for planing and resawing. Electricity was generated on site to provide power and light.

An impressive timber clad building, known as Tanner's barn, stood near the Fullbridge until 1971. It indicates the presence of an industry which needed a copious supply of water in the vicinity.

With Fullbridge closed for repairs in the 1960s, the White Hart and the Welcome Sailor appear very quiet. The Welcome Sailor closed in 1963 but reopened in the 1980s after a spell as offices for Brush the gravel merchants. The White Hart closed permanently in the early 1970s.

The group of men stand outside the shop belonging to A.J. Dykes while the windows of the White Hart are being cleaned, further up the hill on the right is the Ship Hotel. Opposite, with the words 'good stabling' on its side wall, is the White Lion which closed in 1910.

Looking down Market Hill in 1905, the buildings on the left are Hillside apartments, which were formerly part of the Maldon Union until 1873. Directly opposite is a small greengrocer's shop which, with the adjoining property, was demolished in the 1930s. Below this is the butchers shop belonging to W.R. Blaxall, whose delivery trap is outside.

Outside Blaxall's shop whilst descending Market Hill, a traction engine belonging to Mr A. Houghton, a coal merchant on the Causeway, crashed causing extensive damage to the neighbouring house, No. 24 Market Hill. The traction engine had been on hire at Sadd's delivering timber.

The spanking new Bentall car built in Heybridge and purchased by Mr Harold Granger of Hill House, here in the capable hands of chauffeur Tebble in 1911.

Hill House, an imposing building on Market Hill, was the home of Alfred Granger Sadd in 1894. In 1910 Harold Granger, a successful marker gardener, lived here with his family. He was most active in civic affairs being an alderman and upon his death, in 1937, he left the house to the Maldon Borough Council who used it as offices until the council was abolished in 1974.

In the grounds of Hill House stood the Rest, a home for young women founded by Miss Henrietta Sadd to provide holidays for poor London women including the match girls, who worked at the Bryant and May factory at Stratford. Judging by the size of its open upper windows it appears to have adopted the sanatorium practice of exposure to fresh air.

Mr Harold Granger and Mrs Isabelle Granger, their daughters Isabelle and Brynhild together with Miss Henrietta Sadd. All were active in the affairs of the Congregational church in Maldon and the surrounding district.

During the First World War, Mrs Granger was responsible for organising the Girls Patriotic League who performed concerts to entertain troops and raise money for relief work.

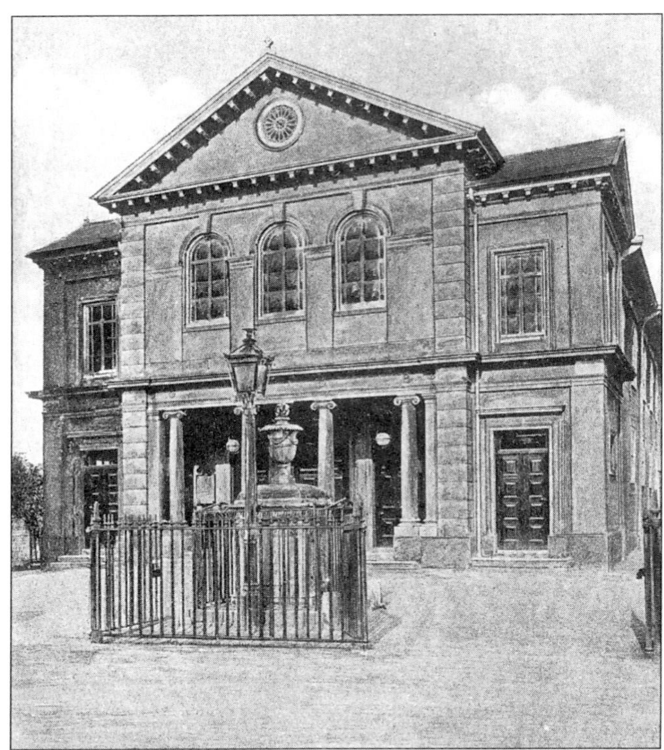

Maldon Congregational church stands on the site of the first Meeting House of Joseph Billio which was erected in 1696. The building depicted dates from 1801 having been enlarged and renovated subsequently until it could seat 900 people. For nearly 200 years this church benefited from the help of the Sadd family.

This group of children have assembled on the site of the British schools. The head gear seems to indicate that this is a Sunday School outing. In 1912 the British Schools pupils moved to the new elementary school in Wantz Road.

Two

Down the High Street to Mill Road

A group of children pose on the corner of Market Hill and the High Street for the photographer.

This view shows the tower of St Peter's church which collapsed in 1664 damaging the nave. Dr Thomas Plume, a Maldonian by birth who enjoyed success as a fashionable cleric in Greenwich in the late seventeenth century, financed the rebuilding of the tower and in 1704 bequeathed his working library to the town. This was to be housed in the upper floor of the two storey building and the lower floor was to be used as a free school.

A view from the top of the tower shows, in the foreground, Church House which was the home of Edward Bright, the fatman of Maldon, who died in 1750 at the age of 29, weighing 44 stone. At the time of this photo in the late 1930s it was the home and surgery of Dr Henry Reynolds Brown. The shops on the far side of the High Street are Britacies, A. Brooks, fishmonger, Burrells, boot and shoe shop, Turners, house furnishers and Caters, radio engineers.

A traffic policeman mans Market Hill corner in this early 1930s view. A plaque can be seen in the churchyard wall recording the widening of the road in 1920. To the right are the shops of A. Hardy-King, draper and newspaper vendor and A.J. Appleby, bootseller.

A portrait of Henry Percy Eve who ran a watch-making and jewellery business at No. 82 High Street. He had taken the business over from his father, Charles Eve, in 1910.

A view of the High Street before 1927 shows the Swan Hotel on the left hand side and past it the attractive house which became Wenlocks the Drapers in 1936. On the opposite side can be seen the high facade of the Hippodrome which had been built before 1910 for dramatic and variety entertainments into which early moving picture shows were incorporated.

In 1927 the Hippodrome was extensively altered and, as shown, became a far more substantial building with an impressive awning extending over the pavement. When the cinema was demolished in the 1960s it became the very first High Street branch of Tesco's. On the right is Baden Saville's wireless shop and Goddard's refreshment rooms. On the left beyond the bus stop is Wenlock's, as opened in 1936, bearing the sign 'Wool and Silk Shop' at No. 85 High Street.

From 1870 No. 85 had been the private house of Joseph Sadler who was a sailmaker with premises on the Hythe. He was elected Councillor in 1885 and was Mayor in 1888 when the branch line to Wickford from Maldon via Woodham Ferrers was opened. He was jeered at and pelted with mud by an angry mob on returning from the opening ceremony at Southend as there had been no celebrations at Maldon.

Bill Raven had completed fifty-nine years of employment at the sail lofts of Taylor's on the Hythe Quay when this photo was taken in the 1950s. Joseph Sadler had handed the business over to his manager Arthur Taylor in 1919.

The tower of St Mary's church which dates from 1300 and traditionally served as a beacon for mariners, looms over the cottages of Church Street. Most of the houses on the right side were demolished in the 1930s.

An interior view of St Mary's after the completion of Fred Chancellor's restoration of 1886 but before his son Wykeham was commissioned to design the reredos, a new altar and to replace the plain East window with a stained one.

St Mary's church in 1885 when it had become very dilapidated. The flue pipes from the combustion stoves can be clearly seen.

Whilst the claim for it to be the oldest church in Essex cannot be substantiated, St Mary's is certainly of Saxon origins. The fine lines of Fred Chancellor's restored St Mary's are to be appreciated. A new south aisle with a transept at the east end of it was built with a new roof for the nave and chancel.

St Mary's church borders the Marine Parade or Promenade where teas are provided as shown in this view from the 1920s.

The church stands on an eminence above the Hythe Quay and the sheds of Walter Cook and Sons boatyard.

This delightful view of Maldon pre-dates the 1895 development of the new Marine Parade. Barges moored at the quay are drying their sails. Bathing machines are in evidence, probably belonging to Benjamin Handley of the Hythe.

A postcard view dated 1907 shows the steam boat *Annie* in mid-channel with day sailing boats and rowing boats, both of which were available for hire below the bath wall.

A lightly laden spritsail barge passes Meter's Head which was a favourite bathing place. Local information useful to visitors' published in 1905, the year that this card was sent, warns that bathing without drawers or other necessary dress was prohibited.

A fleet of seven fishing smacks lie in the foreshore in this 1920's postcard view, including MN7 *Grace Darling* belonging to the Wright family.

A mix of fishing and pleasure vessel including MN15 *William*.

S.S. *Annie* moored off the Hythe Quay out of season. She belonged to Mr F.N. Charrington of the brewery family who out of conscience had established a treatment centre for alcoholics on Osea Island and *Annie* was required to work a daily service to and from the island during the summer months.

She was powered by steam and was licensed to carry 151 passengers. In addition to daily trips she occasionally ran longer sea trips and moonlight trips when her awnings would be hung with lanterns.

Annie proved very popular and continued to run up until the outbreak of the First World War when she was moored out of commission off Osea Island. During this time many parts of her engine went missing.

After the war under new ownership she was fitted with a petrol paraffin engine and renamed the *Maldon Annie*. She continued to work trips on the Blackwater until 1925 when she was moved to the London river to go between Westminster and Greenwich. In 1940 she became one of the little ships taking part in the evacuation of Dunkirk; a journey from which she never returned. Mr Charrington would not have approved of the flag flying in this postcard view of 1920.

The future fishermen and bargemen of Maldon survey the scene around 1906. The large building on the left of the skyline is St Mary's rectory.

The rectory is also visible in this scene. A fleet of day boats are moored just off the beach.

The Marine Lake was completed in 1905 when a creek running behind the Bath Wall was blocked forming a lake 700 feet long by 200 feet wide. Bathing sheds were erected for changing but in this view it also appears bathing machines are in use.

The lake, which was deserted in early spring, became alive with people in high summer as depicted in the card sent in August 1912.

The popularity of the Marine Lake continued through the years. In this 1927 card Bath Cottage can be seen standing on the edge of the creek that was blocked to form the lake. It was used as a bath house before this under the proprietorship of Mr Benjamin Handley.

A tranquil scene on an overcast day just before the outbreak of the Second World War. A sailing barge is moored at the Hythe Quay and the Jolly Sailor advertises Daniell's ales.

Diving boards were always popular and diving contests were a feature of the swimming galas held here but they were removed in the late sixties, following a serious accident.

Donkey rides were a must for visitors but this ride was special in that all the jockeys were barge skippers competing on an alternative means of transport at Carnival time.

No visit to the Marine Parade would have been complete without an ice-cream or glass of lemonade. Sweets and sugared almonds stand in glass jars waiting to be weighed out. This stall belonged to Volta's who also had had premises in the High Street selling confectionery and refreshments since 1906. This view is on a postcard of 1908.

Two elegant ladies appear to be purposefully promenading in this postcard from 1921. 'Maldon is a charming place, seaside and country combined', writes the sender.

The fine gates into the Marine Parade or Promenade as it is now more usually known record the opening by the Mayor Edward A. Fitch on 26 June 1895.

This attractive timbered building was erected next to the gates in 1915. Known as the Promenade Lodge, it will hopefully become the permanent home of the Maldon District museum this year. (E.R.O.)

St Mary's School was erected in 1874 as an infant school. In 1905 it had an average daily attendance of 111 pupils, under the headship of Miss Augusta Flambe.

By 1913 the school had closed with the opening of the new elementary school in Wantz Road and the building had become St Mary's parish room.

Here it is set for a formal meal, unfortunately details of the occasion are not known.

From 1912 until 1983, No. 2 Mill Lane was a sub-post office. Before this, it was the home of Walter Strutt, one of the principal straw and hay merchants in Maldon who also owned several sailing barges to convey his produce to London. It is now the premises of 'All Books'.

Three
Up the High Street to London Road

Playing ball at Wantz Corner in the early 1920s. A petrol pump can be seen on the left below an advertising banner. On the right just before the Rose and Crown is the awning of the marine store, M. & J. Cole and nearer the camera the awning of the Ball's family fishmonger shop which still trades at this site.

The nearest shop on the left is Hazelton's fancy repository followed by Parson's boot dealer and Wiseman's fruitiers. The date of this view is 1910.

The tall building on the left is the Masonic Hall. It previously had been described as the Assembly Room and was the meeting place in 1906 of the Christadelphians. Next to it is the premises of E. Wallis, bootmaker and further up the street is the Hippodrome.

In the foreground adjoining the Swan Hotel is the impressive double-fronted house which belonged to Edwin May, insurance agent. It was here that the fire appliance belonging to the Suffolk and Essex Insurance Company was kept until the early years of the twentieth century. A helmet from the Suffolk and Essex Brigade is in the museum collection. Further up the High Street is the many fronted building belonging to Hick's corn and seed merchants.

The museum occupied the first floor premises above James and George Matthew's for twenty years until 1990. The young lady at the entrance door in this 1973 view now brings her own children to visit the museum.

Children with a hoop stand outside Archer's millinery and Mantle House. Opposite them are the premises of Bentall & Son, draper and outfitter. Many of the buildings on the right between the Moot Hall and Archer's were destroyed in a huge fire on the night of 17 January 1892.

The damaged buildings were rebuilt, the last being the mock-tudor style of the new post office in 1909. The railings above the Moot Hall canopy were added in 1905.

A view from before 1892. The bracketed clock on the Moot Hall had been presented by in 1881 Mr George Courtauld who became the last MP for the Borough of Maldon, in 1891. The shop on the far right belonged to Mr J. Tiffen who was a bootmaker, next to this was the International Tea Stores.

The horse bus, last seen at Maldon East station, has arrived at the King's Head in this view from before 1905. The driver was Mr Arthur Cunningham who was well known for his ability to dislodge small boys hitching a lift on the back stop of the vehicle by dextrous use of his long horse whip. The building on the right belonged to the London and County Bank at the time.

This splendid view is said to have been taken by a Maldonian on flying training in the Second World War and shows the patchwork of small buildings and gardens lying behind the High Street. The Friary buildings can be seen in the centre top with All Saints' vicarage, the Bell and the Blue Boar along the lower part of the photograph. The large building next to the Moot Hall is the Public Hall which could accommodate 600 people for entertainments. It was used as a corn exchange and had originally housed the Maldon literary and mechanics institutes, latterly it became the GPO sorting offices.

This relaxed portrait shows the Mayor and Mayoress, Councillor and Mrs H.W. Sadd with corporation and borough officials in the mayoral year 1911-1912. Front row, from left to right - Aldermen E.A. Fitch, C.E. Barritt, the Mayor and Mayoress, Aldermen H.A. Krohn and G. Wade. Second row - W.H. DeCaen (accountant), Councillors T.J. Turner, G.D. Handley and F.W. Moss, F.H. Bright (Town Clerk) W.J. Brown (asst clerk), Councillors C.S. Goodey, E.T. Baker and behind is H. Granger. Third row - T.R. Swales (surveyor), Sergeant Mace J. Coult, Councillors F.Bawtree, T.E. Hayes, and J.E. Freeman. Fourth row - S.H.T. Crabb (auditor), T.H. Barbrook (port sanitary inspector), Councillor J.J. Furlong.

Until 1912 the lower floor of the Moot Hall served as a police station. In 1910 an inspector and four constables were stationed here. The panel to the left of the principal door could be broken and the hour bell of the clock rung to summon members of the fire brigade in the event of a fire.

In this view of c. 1950 shops occupied by Bee's florist and Pooles press are on the left. The King's Head, behind its eighteenth century porch, was flourishing.

A bath chair adds to the traffic in the High Street around 1900. The block of houses behind the trees on the left, Nos 27-33 High Street, were demolished to open up the view of All Saints' church sometime after 1916.

A postcard view dated October 1911 to Alice of Winchmore Hill arranging to meet her on the following Sunday in the gateway where the dog is standing. At that time it was a carriage entrance through the building but is now incorporated in the bank premises.

This charming portrait of Alderman T.J. Turner and his family was taken around 1913 in the Glendale Studio, 8 Market Hill. His daughter Winifred was highly commended some ten years later when she and her fiancé rescued a visitor from drowning while out rowing on the river.

Alderman Turner ran a clothiers and general outfitters at No. 66 High Street from 1902, eventually expanding to take over No. 64. The business was still in operation until the premises was demolished and a supermarket built on the site in 1971. (E.R.O.)

Opposite at No. 43 High Street, Henry Leech took over an ironmongery business in 1902 which continued under that name until the premises were incorporated into a new post office building in the 1980s.

Stan and Edna Sparks behind the counter at H.G. Leech's shop shortly before it closed. Mr Leech's daughters were sadly killed in an air disaster in the 1960s. Their memorial is their garden off London Road, which was given to the Borough Council.

All Saint's church before 1892 showing its unique triangular tower with a hexagonal spire. The cottages still stand in front of it on the right. In 1858 three more cottages would have blocked this view, their sites were given to the church in that year.

All Saints' church. The large south door appears to be a regular means of access with the wide path leading from a narrow opening into the High Street.

The interior of All Saints' prior to the erection of the rood screen in 1925 and the replacement of the pulpit in 1951.

The interior of the D'Arcy chapel showing the rich wall arcading of the fourteenth century long before the Washington window presented by the citizens of Maldon, Massachusetts had been installed in 1928.

A war memorial bearing 146 names was unveiled in May 1921 on the site of the demolished shops.

A 1930s view in which the war memorial and the water trough given, 'In memory of a good mother who lived and died in this town', can be seen. The intricate wrought iron inn sign advertising the Shrimp brand beers and the railings outside 'Stonecroft', a private residence on the right, are a feature of Maldon.

Further ornate inn signs are shown at the Blue Boar and across the road at the Bell Inn. The latter pub closed in 1958 and is now a private residence.

Fifteenth century buildings forming the bars of the Blue Boar, seen here in 1951.

Five wagons loaded with Sunday School children and hampers await the signal to leave on a sunny afternoon in 1913. The destination of the outing would be Baddow Rodney with a first stop at The Oak at Woodham Mortimer for ginger beer and lemonade.

Baddow Rodney was a pleasure ground related to the Rodney Inn, in an area now known as Heather Hills.

The beginning of the High Street with the steps leading to 'Oakwood', the home of the Ortewell family. The railed area on the opposite side of the road was a garden belonging to 'Oakwood'. The shops J. Gower, confectioner, G. Smith, tobacconists and Dedman, stationer, can be identified which would date the view to around 1890.

The purpose-built police station was erected on the site of the Orttewells front garden in 1912.

Maldon's much loved gas lamps disappeared from the street scene in 1972. These examples stood in London Road. Gas was supplied by the Maldon Gas Light Company's works in the High Street, which was first established in 1839.

In 1910 members of the 'Sadd' family lived in London Road and Beeleigh Road. Here young members of the family Betty, Marjorie, Gladys and Olive are in the trap with Norman leading the donkey who was called Seamus.

A fine portrait of Harry William Sadd in the uniform of Superintendent of the Fire Brigade, c. 1894. He occupied this position for five years and was in the crew that attended the 'Great Fire' in Maldon High Street in 1892.

The Maldon fire brigade with their Merryweather steam fire engine outside the headquarters in London Road, c. 1911. The Captain, Stephen Tydeman, is standing in the centre while on his right in the cap and civilian clothes is Mr F.W. Moss, headmaster of Maldon British Schools. It was in a room above the fire station that the Maldon museum was first established in 1923, going into storage when this part of the building was demolished in 1938 to make way for a new station.

Many visitors to Maldon in the 1940s and '50s would have made use of the youth hostel in West Chase which was opened in Easter 1938.

The cemetery, with its two chapels of rest, was founded in 1855 and enlarged in 1883. It seems an unusual choice of subject for a postcard. The house to the right is Wintersleet Farm.

Four
From Beeleigh to Heybridge

The mill stream, which powered the water-wheels of Beeleigh mill, was filled in during the 1960s. The mill itself had been destroyed by fire in 1875.

This view shows the Tudor additions built after the dissolution of Beeleigh Abbey in 1540. In 1912 the Baker family, who owned the Abbey, leased it to Captain F. Grantham who embarked on restoration work which has been continued by Miss Christina Foyle, the present owner.

The older parts of the Abbey are shown in this view from the east, including the Canons' dormitory and parlour above a warming room and the chapter house.

The opening scene of a pageant staged at Beeleigh Abbey in 1936 is one of a series of photographs taken by Cyril Osborne.

St Norbet, founder of the 'White Canons', who established the Abbey in 1180, is depicted in this further scene from the pageant in which many of the parts were played by local teachers.

The avenue of trees leading to Beeleigh Falls with the Falls House visible in the background, c. 1890. To the left is the oddly shaped elm tree, which was known as the lion tree.

The resemblance to a lion's head was sufficient to frighten generations of children. Sadly, the tree was in poor condition and its upper part had to be felled shortly after the First World War, the remainder surviving until the 1930s.

The long weir at Beeleigh, with its waterfall, provided a popular scenic attraction visited throughout the year. This card was posted on 31 December 1907.

In the summer months fishing was enjoyed in the waters of the River Blackwater above the weir. Water can be seen flowing over the Beeleigh lock gates in the background on the left marking the point from which the cut from the River Chelmer to the River Blackwater was made by the Navigation Company.

Young anglers occupy a favoured fishing position hoping especially for a catch of bream. The brick bridge in the background carries the track from Langford to the golf club.

The Maldon golf course was established in 1891, between the Navigation and the River Chelmer. The professional at the time this card was sent was Mr Walter James, who served the Maldon Golf Club from 1902 until 1935.

In 1888 The Great Eastern Railway constructed a branch line from Maldon to Woodham Ferrers. Construction of embankments and a brick bridge over the Chelmer and Blackwater Navigation Canal combined to make this a costly venture.

A bow string viaduct supported by brick towers carried the railway over the tidal River Chelmer. An extensive cutting was then dug taking the line through to Maldon West station.

The classic skyline of Maldon. From left to right, the Congregational church, St. Peter's tower, the Moot Hall and All Saints tower. In the foreground is the canal with the River Chelmer beyond it.

Cattle are drinking from the gently sloping bank of the River Blackwater, which then bends to the right to feed Heybridge mill, which is just visible through the trees. The Navigation Canal continues towards the Black Bridge at Heybridge.

This view shows the new canal bridge installed in 1910. Known as the Wave bridge, a name derived from the neighbouring ale house, it carried the road towards Goldhanger. The ornamental palisading on either side of the bridge, bearing the Essex crest in its centre, was specially manufactured at Maldon Iron Works. To the right are the buildings of Going's wharf. Joseph Going was a merchant ship owner who lived at Heybridge Basin in 1870. Rowing skiffs for hire are moored close by. The large building towering above the wharf is the warehouse built by E.H. Bentall in 1863.

A horse drawn barge can be seen heading for Heybridge Basin on the Navigation Canal as it runs a straight course from the Wave Bridge.

A dramatic scene at Heybridge mill in 1928 as water pours up the River Blackwater flooding the surrounding area. After the severe floods of 1953 the river was dammed but Heybridge mill was demolished in 1955.

Looking back from Wave Bridge, the Navigation Canal can be seen skirting the works of Edward Hammond Bentall and Co, iron founders and agricultural implement manufacturers. Edward's father, William, had established the factory here by 1815, to manufacture the cast iron plough that he had perfected first at Goldhanger. He was attracted by the canal which had been completed in 1797.

A poignant scene of a funeral barge heading from the Basin towards the canal side Heybridge cemetery. The funeral was that of a young seaman drowned in the sea-lock following a fall from his vessel. His father sits in the bows, before the coffin, with the top hatted undertaker. Relatives and residents of the Basin, including six men permanently available as pall-bearers when required, surround the coffin. At the helm is Ned Woodcraft who, on his death, is reputed to have been the last person to be transported in this way.

A tree-lined path edges the canal. These trees were willows from whose wood cricket bats were made, providing an important source of revenue for the Navigation Company.

Here the willows can be seen along the far bank. Many craft, both pleasure and working, are moored including a wooden canal barge.

A steam ship is moored in the basin opposite the range of buildings on Lock Hill. The furthest building is the Old Ship Inn which was known as the Chelmer Brig when it was owned by the Navigation Company.

The gates into the sea-lock are seen in the foreground with the lock-keeper's house on the left. The Basin could accommodate vessels of up to 300 tons but in this view only a two masted ship and two spritsail barges are moored. The building which housed perishable cargoes for the Navigation Company is on the right.

Heybridge Hall is a seventeenth century house, which was once the home of the Freshwater and Hering families, whose monuments are to be found in the parish church.

St Andrew's church, Heybridge, is of Norman origin but much modified over the centuries with a foreshortened tower and lowered nave, the results of past tidal floodings causing the upper part to fall.

A charabanc outing of the 1920s pauses outside the Anchor in Heybridge Square. The party aboard is reputed to be members of the Warren Golf Club in Woodham Walter.

A water sprinkling cart laying the dust is seen passing between the Half Moon Inn. The Anchor Inn on the left belonged to the Chelmsford Brewery.

Heybridge Street at the turn of the century with the shop of A. Harris, seed merchant, on the left. In the background are the buildings of Heybridge iron works and St Andrew's In Memoriam School, erected in 1869 in remembrance of a former vicar. The school was closed in 1900 and became the Waring Rooms.

In 1875 Edward Hammond Bentall built terraces of cottages for his work force in Heybridge. Each cottage was separated by a wide path, known as a lane, from its individual wash house with a garden beyond. The wash house contained a brick built copper, a large sink and a wooden seated closet with a galvanised pail beneath. Water had to be carried from communal taps. As with Mr Bentall's own home, shown on page 91, the cottages were built from concrete and as originally constructed had flat roofs, being known locally as 'flat tops'. Pitched roofs were added by 1918. On the death of Hammond Bentall's great grandson, Ernest, the cottages were put up for auction in 1930, when they could be purchased for under £100. Les Saye's photograph shows Woodfield cottages in 1970.

Hunter's Garage was erected at the end of the Causeway in 1929, replacing a cycle repair shop. This 1938 picture shows Mr Frederick Came, the chief mechanic, and Mr Harry King.

The official reopening of the Heybridge branch of the Maldon and Heybridge Co-op society, which was situated at the junction of Colchester and Hall Roads.

Around 1890 a windmill still stood on Mill Beach but only two of its sails remained.

The popularity of Mill Beach is evident in this post Second World War view. The Mill Beach Hotel and Restaurant, licensed since 1894, provided hospitality for visitors.

In 1905 Osea Island was being developed as a pleasure and health resort by its owner, Mr F.N. Charrington. A regular summer steamboat service provided access to its shingle and sand beach.

The water cart calling at the Old Farm House and cottages on Osea, at the turn of the century.

Feeding the chickens at Osea Farm. Osea is a true island connected by a causeway, which is covered by the tide. It was noted for the many wild fowl which gathered around its shores at certain times of the year, attracting gentlemen from London, who enjoyed shooting as a pastime.

Edward Hammond Bentall, the principal employer in Heybridge, had a splendid Italianate house built for himself here in 1873, known as The Towers. A pioneering form of construction, with concrete blocks as the major building materials, was used. The setting for the houses was enhanced by the formation of a lake in its grounds.

The interior of the house was sumptuously decorated. Ducted hot air was used for heating as there were no fire places built, although some were subsequently added. Its construction presented some difficulty to its demolition in the 1950s.

Bentall, having perfected a petrol engine for agricultural use went into motor car production in the early years of the twentieth century. Unfortunately due to the size of the cylinders used, they fell foul of the Government's horse power tax and only one hundred vehicles were completed. A two-seater model is seen standing by a concrete wall favoured by the Bentall family.

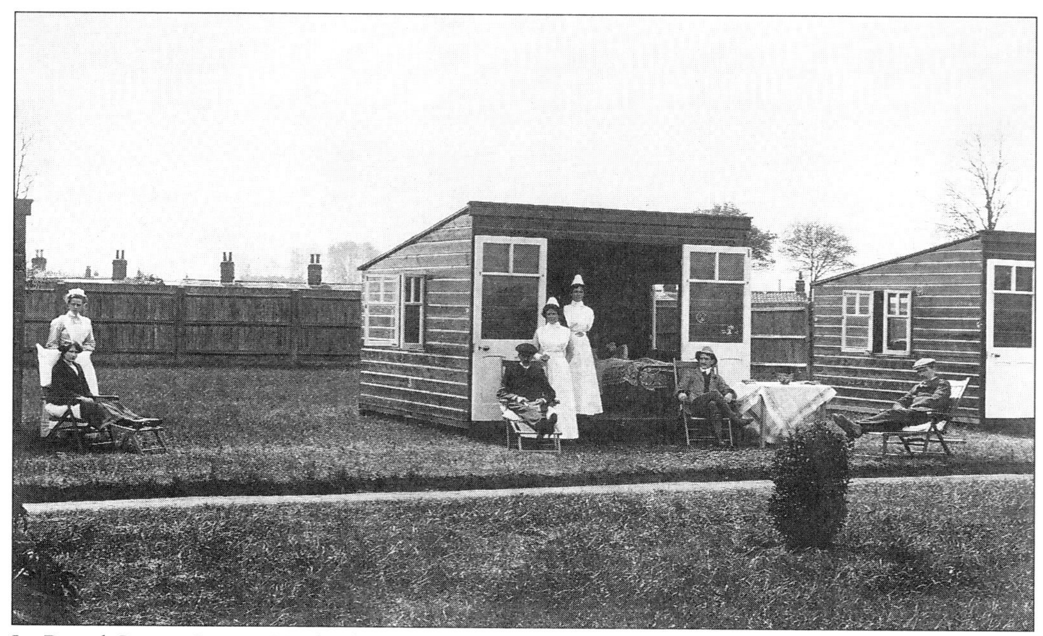

In Broad Street Green, Heybridge, an isolation hospital was built in 1903 providing, initially, accommodation for only ten beds.

Five

Highways and Byways

The Causeway, seen here as an elegant tree-lined avenue, was the ancient route from Heybridge to Maldon, across Potman Marsh.

Spital Road was, in ancient times, the link between the centre of Maldon and the hospital for lepers, dedicated to St Giles. Handsome villas line the road and cattle are seen on the right coming from refreshment at the Ware Pond. E.R.O.

The gates of the workhouse, or union, are seen on the right of this picture of Spital Road. The workhouse was purpose-built in 1873 and is now St Peter's hospital.

In August 1917, the Bate family pose seated in a model T. Ford within their motor sales room, situated in Spital Road.

Maldon West station, opened in 1888, was on the branch line to Woodham Ferrers. The booking office was at road level with stairs giving access to the platforms which were in a deep cutting below.

Maldon Grammer School was opened in Fambridge Road in 1907. Designed as a mixed school and pupil teachers centre, the hall and library wing were added in 1932.

Maldon Grammar School. The Headmaster, Mr S.G. Deed M.A, who held the post from 1912 until 1939, sits surrounded by members of staff and pupils in May 1932. Mrs Deed is on his right, then Mr D.W. Downs, Mr Knowles, Mrs F. Cowell, Miss Martin, Miss Smith and Miss Dodd. To his left are Mr E.M. Williams, Mr A.C. Edwards, Mr W.H. Bream, Mr T. Turner, Mr W. Berridge and Mr Dynes.

One of the smallest shops in Maldon to disappear in recent times was Bright's cabin in Fambridge Road, pictured here in February 1974.

A portrait of the Wash family of Fambridge Road by Hazeltine Frost, photographer of Market Hill since 1908. Mr Couzens (centre, standing) had married Alice Wash (first row, right) on his return from the Boer War.

Gray's Brewery, situated in Gate Street, which had been producing beer since the early nineteenth century. It closed and was sold to the English Electric Valve Company in 1954.

The location of these elegant houses is Cross Road which links Fambridge Road to Wantz Road and was formerly known as Purleigh Road.

Three storey houses in Wantz Road with the creeper-covered Mizpah, home of rest, seen to the right. The Star Inn is situated further down the road with the bow window of a china and glass shop next to it.

Further down Wantz Road is the Volunteers Arms which closed in 1979. It was named after volunteers serving in the Crimean campaign.

The joys of Maldon, including rowing, sailing, bathing, reading and dog exercising are promoted on the cover of this brochure for an auction of plots on which villas could be built. Apart from two houses in Spital Road and a semi-detached villa in Fambridge Road, this estate to the south of Maldon was never built as planned.

Six
The Surrounding Villages

Ulting was one of the smallest parishes in the Maldon Union with a population of 164 people in 1901. It had its own school, established in 1865, which could accomodate up to sixty children.

Langford had its own station which displayed a fine collection of metal signs, mainly for soap. Tickets were sold by the occupant of the cottage which can be seen beyond the platform. Whether she could claim to be the only station mistress in England as noted on the postcard is doubtful!

St Gile's church is noted for its semi-circular west end. The mill building of the 1880s is seen in the background. An earlier mill had been destroyed in a disastrous fire in March 1879.

A 1950s scene of a steam-hauled branch train leaving Wickham Bishop's station for Maldon. Both the station and the water mill belonging to James and George Mathews, seen in the background, were closed in 1964. The mill was demolished in 1975.

This is believed to be a scene of an electioneering party outside Wickham Bishops School in 1906, when it was reported that the 'Liberals had more traps but the Tories had a motor'. This belonged to Mr George Taylor of the 'Beacons', who is standing by the car. The chauffeur leaning nonchalantly on the left is Teddy Newman and the distinguished gentleman in the centre is Mr Robert Fuller, veterinary surgeon. The driver of the trap is Mr Alfred Ward of Totham Hall. Others present are Messrs. Bickmore, Allfrey, Seager and the son of Mr Ward.

In 1904 a branch line was opened by the Great Eastern Railway from Kelvedon to Tollesbury. An intermediate station was provided for Tolleshunt D'Arcy. It had a wooden shed for the waiting room and an old coach body serving as a lockable parcels office.

A street scene in Great Totham including the Weslyan Methodist chapel, cottages of varying age and a windmill for grinding corn.

Much time must have been spent in the early years of this century in having haircuts, a rarely photographed activity. Here in Great Totham the barber, Bill Spurling, cuts the hair of a young member of the Thynn family. Other members await their turn including Bill Thynn, the father, whilst the mother and the latest addition watch from the window. The elderly gentleman on crutches is Mr Seales.

Alms houses were erected in Great Totham in 1855, to house three married couples and three widows. One of these ladies is Mrs Pratt but the names of the others are unknown.

Steam threshing at Tolleshunt Major on the site of what was to become Goldhanger Fruit Farms. The threshing machine and elevator are powered by the belt of the traction engine.

A portable steam engine at work with its driver and fireman to the left of the picture. They and the equipment would be provided by contractors to the farms. Despite the introduction of machinery a large labour force was still required.

Tending the chickens at Tolleshunt Major while a horse-drawn rake leans against the shed.

A crowded beach scene at Goldhanger. This is probably a swimming gala with seven contestants in the water and a crowd of school fellows and parents watching the event.

The picturesque inn, The Bell at Woodham Walter, is said to have been built in 1566, the same year as the church. One landlord in the early nineteenth century, additionally worked as a cobbler in the small room to the right of the main building.

The Street, Woodham Walter, looking towards the forge and brook, is shown on this card which was sent in 1915.

This scene of Mr Ratcliff's farm was captured on film in September 1973 by John Osborne, the well known local artist. It shows Mr Hugh Saunders and 'Club' dung carting on the farm which is situated at Hoe mill between Woodham Walter and Beeleigh.

The Oak at Woodham Mortimer originally stood close to some fine oak trees but continues to serve the public as the Royal Oak. E.R.O.

The tiny lathe and plaster church of St Nicholas, Hazeleigh, stood by Hazeleigh Hall until demolished in August 1922. As depicted in this water colour, it was falling into a ruinous state.

An extremely rare photograph of the interior of St Nicholas, showing the box pews, reading desk and pulpit. It was recorded in 1905 that the floors sloped some nine inches from the aisle to the south wall, as can be seen here.

The delivery van from Bunting's butchers shop in Maldon High Street is seen calling at cottages in Howe Green near Purleigh around 1930. It is guarded by an ever hopeful dog.

Howe Green is at the southern end of the parish of Purleigh, where an area of common land still exists. The name of the farm is derived from two saxon words 'Leah' and 'hoh'. The farm house has been much modified since this card was produced around 1910.

An extensive range of timber-framed, timber-clad cottages line the street at Latchingdon. Opposite are the village shops and beyond them, the Red Lion.

The central part of this building, Valley House, dates from the early eighteenth century. In the nineteenth century it was extended to the right with an extension becoming a seperate dwelling. The small addition to the left and the single storey building in the background formed Brown's grocery store and bakery.

A charity school was established in Purleigh in 1800, situated in a class room behind behind the school house, which was given to the community by the rector John Eveleigh. Additional classrooms were added in 1817 and 1872. In 1900 the average attendence was seventy-six children.

The charity school closed on the opening of the council school in 1915. It was built to accomodate 150 children. It is shown here with the new school house in a postcard sent in 1931.

The Bell is seen on the right of this postcard view of 1926 with a pond in the foreground, situated surprisingly near the top of the steep church hill. The centre building includes the village shop and post office.

The large thatched barn belonging to Purleigh Hall was converted into two dwellings in 1984. It was erected around 1770 using some much older materials and was unusual in having two wagon entrances. The tower of All Saints' church can be seen behind the brick built calf sheds. To the right is a rear view of The Bell.

Seven

Days to Remember

In the fine summer of 1913 the 4th, 5th, 6th and 7th territorial battalions of the Essex regiment arrived for their annual camp, which in that year was just to the south of Maldon. Here a group assemble in the station yard at Maldon West.

Led by a military brass band the men were marched over the railway bridge preceeded by a policeman and two railway staff members. Nearly 2,500 men and 100 officers were encamped on this occasion.

Many interested Maldonians, including several potential recruits, mingle with the military en route to the camp. By May 1914 the local G company was over strength but this did not prevent Sergeant Instructor Shonk observing, on the occasion of the opening of new headquarters, that there were many young fellows standing about in the streets who did not play football, or cricket, or appear to have any interest in anything. He felt their physical condition would be remarkably improved after a short period of drills.

A cycling corps of the Essex Regiment had been formed and was in attendance at the camp. This group included Maldonians H.A. and T.W. Bate who ran the Maldon cycle company. During the First World War the cycling corps was principally involved in local coastal defence work.

On each day of the two week camp, one or sometimes two battalions would march through town to the Marine Parade to swim in the lake but on this occasion they were to be reviewed in full dress uniform. This street scene also shows Mr Oxley Finch, the fishmonger, standing outside his shop, beside which the passage leads through to All Saints' church. In the right foreground are the aproned staff of the Central Meat Company.

The territorials, with a mounted field officer, await review on the recreation ground at the Marine Parade. The large house in the background is St Mary's rectory.

Troops were conveyed to and from the camp by special trains to Maldon West. Here they are preparing to embark from the Up platform. The volume of traffic at this period was the greatest the station saw from the time of opening in 1880 to its closure to passengers in September 1939.

On the night of Friday 16 April 1915 the engines of a German Zeppelin were heard to be approaching from the direction of the river. It appeared to hover over the workhouse building in Spital Road and dropped more than twenty bombs, both explosive and incendiary which fell within a square mile of each other. One of the incendiary bombs was recovered and subsequently a china reproduction was made by the W.H. Goss company bearing the crest of Maldon.

One of the explosives fell at the back of Mr Henry Foreman's house at No. 21 Spital Road, destroying his workshop and a neighbouring iron shed belonging to Mr Arthur Smith, a builder. The side wall of No. 25 Spital Road was badly damaged, shrapnel passing two feet above the bed of the occupant, Mr Walter Mott, supervisor at the post office.

Many tiles were dislodged on properties near to the explosion and all the windows in Mount Pleasant were broken. A bag of tools from Mr Smith's shed were found in a garden one hundred yards away.

In a nearby meadow, another explosive bomb had made a crater five feet deep. Troops of the 2nd battalion of the 8th Worcestershire regiment, who were billeted in the workhouse, were powerless against the attack. Fortunately there was only one casualty, a speckled hen, belonging to Mr Henry Hutson, dairyman of Gate Street. The *Daily Express* of Saturday 17 April bears the headline 'Baby-killers foiled. Tragic death of a hen. What the Zeppelin accomplished in Essex'. Thus a propaganda victory was claimed!

The coronation of King George V in June 1911 was celebrated with great enthusiasm. Electricity was used to illuminate decorations for the first time and Bentall's entry for the decorated heavy trade carts was not accepted as it was horse-drawn. It was awarded a special prize in a class of its own - the first lorry to appear on such an occasion. It carried a rootpulper, a chaff-cutter, and a 'Goldhanger' plough.

A meeting outside the Maldon and Heybridge Co-operative society's premises at No. 19 Market Hill. The Co-operative had been founded in 1873 by workers at the Maldon iron works. A fine display of ladies hats is seen in the millinery section of the store. The town was decorated for the Coronation.

A procession assembles in the High Street with the town band in Hussars uniform followed by the 2nd Maldon Troop Boy Scouts. The heavy trade cart entry from the Maldon and Heybridge Co-operative society, which gained third prize in the Coronation parade, stands behind.

This card bears the message that it illustrates a garden party at the Maldon vicarage. It appears to date from around 1910 when Reverend Leonard Hughes would have been vicar.

These extremely well costumed highwaymen and a highway lady are assembled outside the Tudor wing of the Blue Boar in 1934. They were collecting money for local hospitals at carnival time. Sadly one highwayman was severely injured in a fall from the running board of a car,

which was being requested to stand and deliver and this method of fundraising was abandoned. It would be marvellous to learn the identities of those shown.

The first lifeboat demonstration in Maldon was on Saturday 27 July 1907 when the Institution life boat No. 8, manned by a Southend crew, was towed down the High Street following a procession of bands and decorated carts. With the Mayor and Mayoress, Councillor and Mrs H.A. Krohn, the Aldermen and Town Clerk safely aboard, it was launched onto the marine lake.

The master of the hunt with a pack of hounds making their way up the High Street to pause outside the Blue Boar, for refreshment. Traditionally this took place on Boxing Day. Both the East Essex and the Essex union hunted locally.

Regatta day at Maldon in 1895, the day the Marine Promenade was opened, with the fishing smack race about to start. Spritsail barges, bedecked with flags are moored to the left of the picture. The well laden vessel in the centre provides a somewhat hazardous grandstand for those aboard.

Christmas Day in the workhouse. On Christmas Day 1915 the inmates of the Maldon poor law institution were treated to this enigmatic tableau with the matron, Mrs Emily White, as Britannia, Mrs Green as Russia, Mrs White junior as Japan, Miss Brown as Italy and the writer of the postcard as France. The identities of the pom-pom decorated gentlemen and the unhappy dog are, mercifully, not disclosed.